BETH HENLEY

MONOLOGUES FOR WOMEN

With love and more love to Lydy Caldwell Becker for sharing
with me her secrets about the power, terror, and beauty of
words, words, words.

Published by
Dramaline Publications, 10470 Riverside Drive, Suite #201
Toluca Lake, CA 91602.

Library of Congress Cataloging-in-Publication Data

Henley, Beth.
    Beth Henley: Monologues for Women.
        p.   cm.   C. /
    Contents: Am I Blue—Crimes of the Heart—The Miss Firecracker Contest—The Wake of Jamey Foster—Debutante Ball—The Lucky Spot—Abundance—Signature.
        ISBN 0-940669-20-X : $6.95
        1. Women—Drama. 2. Monologues. 1. Title.
PS3558.E4962A6   1992b
812'.54—dc20
808.8

Cover design by John Sabel.

This book is printed on 55# Glatfelter acid-free paper, a paper that meets the requirements of the American National Standard of Permanence of paper for printed library material.

CONTENTS

INTRODUCTION

In performing these monologues, I would like to share the idea of hope. I feel all of these women are compelled and foiled, tortured and exalted by the never ending affliction of hope. Thus they are never tepidly depressed—they are despairingly anguished. (Lenny, Meg, Marshael, Bess, Carnelle.) They are not silly, sweet, or stupid—they are alive with burning poetic vision. (Babe, Pixrose, Popeye, Macon, Violet.) Even the characters who lack a certain spiritual enlightenment (Katty, Elain, L-Tip) are to me compelling in their dogged need to glorify the endless minutiae of everyday life and avoid their deep terror of being isolated and unworthy of love.

In short, let me say that I care for all of the women in this book. Having been deep inside their skin, I have had the exhilaration of experiencing each of them in a visceral, three-dimensional way. I understand them and, thus, I treasure them and learn from them. I do hope that, if you choose to become one of these women, that you will fearlessly embrace her and illuminate her with your own dangerous, magical, real deep self, self.

Beth Henley

Los Angeles, 1992.

AM I BLUE
(Set in New Orleans.)

Am I Blue was presented by the Circle Repertory Company, in New York City, on January 10, 1982. It was directed by Stuart White. The cast was as follows:

John Polk Richards	Jeff McCracken
Ashbe Williams	June Stein
Hilda	Pearl Shear
The Barker	Jimmie Ray Weeks
The Bum	Edward Seamon
The Hippie (Clareece)	Ellen Conway
The Whore	Katherine Cortez

ASHBE

Ashbe gives John Polk some inside information on the prostitute he has an appointment with at midnight.

G. G., that's just her working name. Her real name is Myrtle Reims, she's Kay Reims' older sister. She's, ah, well, Myrtle had acne and there are a few scars left. It's not bad. I think they sort of give her character. Her hair's red only I don't think it's really red. It sort of fizzles out all over her head. She's got a pretty good figure—big top—but the rest of her is kind of skinny.

She was a senior when I was a freshman; so I never really knew her. I remember she used to paint her fingernails lots of different colors—pink, orange, purple. I don't know, but she kind of scares me. About the only time I ever saw her true personality was around a year ago. I was over at Kay's making a health poster for school. Anyway, Myrtle comes busting in screaming about how she can't find her spangled bra anywhere. Kay and I just sat on the floor cutting pictures of food out of magazines while she was storming about slamming drawers and swearing. Finally, she found it. It was pretty garish—red with black and gold sequined G.'s on each cup. That's how I remember the name—G. G.

ASHBE

*Ashbe fantasizes to John Polk about the type of ball she would
like to attend. It is far more elegant than the silly school dance
that is being given this evening, for which she did not have a
date.*

You know we're alike because I don't like dances
either. Well, I like dancing, I just don't like dances.
At least not like—well, not like the one our school
was having tonight...they're so corny.

All they serve is potato chips and fruit punch, and
then this stupid baby band plays and everybody
dances around thinking they're so hot. I frankly
wouldn't dance there. I would prefer to wait till I am
invited to an exclusive ball. It doesn't really matter
which ball, just one where they have huge, golden
chandeliers and silver fountains, and serve delicacies
of all sorts and bubble blue champagne. I'll arrive in
a pink cape. (*Laughing.*) I want to dance in pink!

ASHBE

Ashbe, seeking to align herself with John Polk, reveals her mammoth dislike for the girls at school who exclude her and the orphans from their snobbish clique.

I know what you mean by the kind of girls it's hard to talk to. There are girls a lot that way in the small clique at my school. Really tacky and mean. They expect everyone to be as stylish as they are and they won't even speak to you in the hall. I don't mind if they don't speak to me, but I really love the orphans and it hurts my feelings when they are so mean to them.

They sometimes snicker at the orphans' dresses. The orphans usually have hand-me-down drab ugly dresses. Once Shelly Maxwell wouldn't let Glinda borrow her pencil, even though she had two. It hurt her feelings.

I put spells on the girls in the clique—mostly just voodoo. Here, I'll show you my doll. (*She goes to get the doll and comes back with a straw voodoo doll. Her air as she returns is one of frightening mystery.*) I know a lot about the subject. Cora—she used to wash dishes in the Moonlight Cafe—told me all about voodoo. She's a real expert on the subject, went to all the meetings and everything. Once she caused a man's throat to rot away and turn almost totally black. She's moved to Chicago now.

The thing about voodoo is that both parties have to believe in it for it to work. That's where my main problem comes in. I have to make the clique believe in it, yet I have to be very subtle. Mainly, I give reports in English class or speech.

I don't cast spells that'll do any real harm. Mainly, just the kind of thing to make them think—to keep them on their toes.

CRIMES OF THE HEART
(Set in Hazlehurst, Mississippi.)

Crimes of the Heart was presented on Broadway at the Golden Theatre, on November 10, 1981. It was directed by Melvin Bernhardt. The cast was as follows:

Lenny Magrath	Lizbeth Mackay
Chick Boyle	Sharon Ullrick
Doc Porter	Raymond Baker
Meg Magrath	Mary Beth Hurt
Babe Botrelle	Mia Dillon
Barnette Lloyd	Peter MacNicol

BABE

Babe finally reveals to her sister Meg what compelled her to shoot her own husband in the stomach.

Willie Jay was over. And we were just standing around on the back porch playing with Dog. Well, suddenly, Zackery comes from around the side of the house. And he startled me 'cause he's supposed to be away at the office, and there he is coming 'round the side of the house. Anyway, he says to Willie Jay, "Hey, boy, what are you doing back there?" And I said, "He's not doing anything. You just go on home, Willie Jay! You just run right on home." Well, before he can move, Zackery comes up and knocks him once right across the face and then shoves him down the porch steps, causing him to skin up his elbow real bad on the concrete. Then he says, "Don't you ever come around here again, of I'll have them cut out your gizzard!" Well, Willie Jay starts crying, these tears come streaming down his face, then he gets up real quick and runs away with Dog following off after him. After that, I don't remember too much clearly; let's see...I went on into the living room, and I went right up to the davenport and opened the drawer where we keep the burglar gun...I took it out. Then I—I brought it up to my ear. That's right. I put it right inside my ear. Why, I was gonna shoot off my own head! That's what I was gonna do. Then I heard the back door slamming and suddenly, for some reason, I thought about mama...how she'd hung herself. And here I was about ready to shoot myself.

Then I realized—that's right when I realized how I didn't want to kill myself! And she—she probably didn't want to kill herself. She wanted to kill him, and I wanted to kill him, too. I wanted to kill Zackery, not myself 'cause I—I wanted to live! So I waited for him to come on into the living room. Then I held out the gun, and I pulled the trigger, aiming at his heart, but getting him in the stomach. (*After a pause.*) It's funny that I really did that.

BABE

Babe explains to her lawyer, Barnette Lloyd, what she did immediately after shooting her husband, as they plot her legal defense.

Well, after I shot him, I put the gun down on the piano bench and then I went out into the kitchen and made up a pitcher of lemonade. I made it just the way I like it with lots of sugar and lots of lemon— about ten lemons in all. Then I added two trays of ice and stirred it up with my wooden stirring spoon.

I drank three glasses, one right after the other. They were large glasses, about this tall. Then suddenly, my stomach kind of swoll all up. I guess what caused it was all that sour lemon. Then what I did was...I wiped my mouth off with the back of my hand, like this... (*She demonstrates.*) I did it to clear off all those little beads of water that had settled there. Then I called out to Zackery. I said, "Zackery, I've made some lemonade. Can you use a glass?" He didn't answer.

I poured him a glass anyway and took it out to him. And there he was; lying on the rug. He was looking up at me trying to speak words, I said, "What?...Lemonade?...You don't want it? Would you like a Coke instead?" Then I got the idea, he was telling me to call on the phone for medical help. So I got on the phone and called up the hospital. I gave my name and address and I told them my husband was shot and he was lying on the rug and there was plenty of blood. (*Babe pauses a minute, as Barnette works frantically on his notes.*) I guess that's gonna look kinda bad. Me fixing that lemonade before I called the hospital.

I tell you, I think the reason I made the lemonade, I mean besides the fact that my mouth was bone dry, was that I was afraid to call the authorities. I was afraid. I—I really think I was afraid they would see that I had tried to shoot Zackery, in fact, that I had shot him, and they would accuse me of possible murder and send me away to jail. I mean, in fact, that's what did happen. That's what is happening— 'cause here I am just about ready to go right off to the Parchment Prison Farm. Yes, here I am just practically on the brink of utter doom. Why, I feel so all alone.

BABE

Babe attempts to calm Lenny by explaining Meg's troubled behavior.

Don't resent Meg. Things have been hard for Meg. After all, she was the one who found Mama.

I tell you, Lenny, after it happened, Meg started doing all sorts of these strange things. For instance, back when we used to go over to the library, Meg would spend all her time reading and looking through this old, black book called *Diseases of the Skin.* It was full of the most sickening pictures you'd ever seen. Things like rotting-away noses and eyeballs drooping off down the sides of people's faces and scabs and sores and eaten-away places all over *all* parts of people's bodies.

Anyway, she'd spend hours and hours just forcing herself to look through this book. Why, it was the same way she'd force herself to look at the poster of crippled children stuck up in the window at Dixieland Drugs. You know, that one where they want you to give a dime. Meg would stand there and stare at their eyes and look at the braces on their little crippled-up legs—then she'd purposely go and spend her dime on a double scoop of ice cream cone and eat it all down. She'd say to me, "See, I can stand it. I can stand it. Just look how I'm gonna be able to stand it."

MEG

Meg confesses the hard times she has been suffering out in Los Angeles to Doc Porter, her old lover.

I don't know, Doc. Things got worse for me. After a while, I just couldn't sing anymore. I tell you, I had one hell of a time over Christmas. I went nuts. I went insane. Ended up in L. A. County Hospital. Psychiatric ward.

I couldn't sing anymore; so I lost my job. And I had a bad toothache. I has this incredibly painful toothache. For days I had it, but I wouldn't do anything about it. I just stayed inside my apartment. All I could do was sit around in chairs, chewing on my fingers. Then one afternoon I ran screaming out of the apartment with all my money and jewelry and valuables and tried to stuff it all into one of those March of dimes collection boxes. That was when they nabbed me. Sad story. Meg goes mad.

MEG

Meg rhapsodizes to her sisters about her glorious night with Doc where, for the first time in her life, she sang just for herself.

Good morning! Good morning! Oh, it's a wonderful morning! I tell you, I am surprised I feel this good. I should feel like hell. By all accounts, I should feel like utter hell! (*She is looking for the glue.*) Where's that glue? This damn heel has broken off my shoe. La, la, la, la, la! Ah, here it is! Now let me just get these shoes off. Zip, zip, zip, zip, zip! Well, what's wrong with you two? My God, you look like doom! (*Babe and Lenny stare helplessly at Meg.*) Oh, I know, you're mad at me 'cause I stayed out all night long. Well; I did.

Oh, Lenny, listen to me, now, everything's all right with Doc. I mean nothing happened. Well, actually a lot did happen, but it didn't come to anything. Not because of me, I'm afraid. (*Smearing glue on her heel.*) I mean, I was out there thinking, "What will I say when he begs me to run away with him? Will I have pity on his wife and those two half-Yankee children? I mean, can I sacrifice their happiness for mine? Yes! Oh, yes! Yes, I can!" But...he didn't ask me. He didn't even want to ask me. Why aren't I miserable! Why aren't I morbid! I should be humiliated! Devastated! Maybe these feelings are coming—I don't know. But for now it was...just such fun. I'm happy. I realized I could care about someone. I could want someone. And I sang! I sang all night long! I sang right up into the trees! But not for Old Granddaddy. None of it was to please Old Granddaddy!

BABE

Babe, having finally discovered the reason her mother hung herself along with the cat, shares the revelation with Meg who has just found Babe with her head stuck in the gas oven.

Meg—I know why she did it. (*With joy.*) Mama. I know why she hung the cat along with her. (*With enlightenment.*) It was because she was afraid of dying all alone.

She felt so unsure, you know, as to what was coming. It seems the best thing coming would be a lot of angels and all of them singing. But I imagine they have high, scary voices and little gold pointed fingers that are as sharp as blades and you don't want to meet 'em all alone. You'd be afraid to meet them all alone. So it wasn't like what people were saying about her hanging the cat. Fact is, she loved that cat. She needed him with her 'cause she felt so all alone.

THE MISS FIRECRACKER CONTEST
(Set in Brookhaven, Mississippi.)

The Miss Firecracker Contest was presented by the Manhattan Theatre Club, in New York City, on May 1, 1984. It was directed by Stephen Tobolowsky. The cast was as follows:

Carnelle Scott	Holly Hunter
Popeye Jackson	Belita Moreno
Elain Rutledge	Patricia Richardson
Delmount Williams	Mark Linn-Baker
Mac Sam	Budge Threlkeld
Tessy Mahoney	Margo Martindale

CARNELLE

Carnelle discusses her family's proclivity for dying tragically to her seamstress Popeye Jackson.

This house is just like my Aunt Ronelle fixed it up. It's got her special touch: this old spinning wheel; these lace doilies; these old pictures in frames here. I'd prefer something more modern and luxurious, but—that's just me.

I used to live here with my aunt but she died. She had cancer. It happened just a few weeks before last Christmas. We were very close. It was a tragedy. (*As she pours Popeye's tea.*) You may of heard about her; Ronelle Williams? It was a famous medical case—ran in all the newspapers. Well, see what it was—Do you take lemon?

Anyway, she had this cancer of the pituitary gland, I believe it was: so what they did was they replaced her gland with the gland of a monkey to see if they could save her life—Just help yourself to the sugar—And they did, in fact, keep her alive for a month or so longer than she was expected to live.

(*Pouring herself some tea.*) Of course, there were such dreadful side effects. She, well, she started growing long, black hairs all over her body just, well, just like an ape. It was very trying. But she was so brave. She even let them take photographs of her.

Everyone said she was just a saint. A saint or angel; one or the other.

It was awfully hard on me losing my Aunt Ronelle— although I guess I should be used to people dying. It seems like people've been dying practically all my life, in one way or another. First my mother passed when I was barely a year old. Then my Daddy kinda drug me around with him till I was about nine and he couldn't stand me any longer; so he dropped me off to live with my Aunt Ronelle and Uncle George and their own two children: Elain and Delmont. They're incredible those two. They're just my ideal. Anyhow, we're happy up until the time when Uncle George falls to his death trying to pull this bird's nest out from the chimney. Tommy Turner was passing by throwing the evening paper and he caught sight of the whole event. Boom.

Anyhow, my original Daddy appears back here to live with us looking kinda fat and swollen. And after staying on with us about two years, he suddenly drops dead in the summer's heat while running out to the Tropical Ice Cream truck. Heart failure, they said it was. Then this thing with Aunt Ronelle dying right before Christmas. It's been hard to bear.

Well, they say everyone's gonna be dying someday. I believe it too.

POPEYE

Popeye concurs with Elain that life is hard. By way of illustration, she tells the heartbreaking story of Sweet Pea and Willas.

I once knew these two midgets by the names of Sweet Pea and Willas. I went to their wedding and they was the only midgets there. Rest a their family was regular size people. But they was so happy together and they moved into a little midget house where everything was mite size like this little old desk they had and this little old stool. Then Sweet Pea got pregnant and later on she had what they called this Caesarean birth where they slice open your stomach and pull the baby out from the slice. Well, come to find out, the baby's a regular size child and soon that baby is just too large for Sweet Pea to carry around and too large for all that mite sized furniture. So Sweet Pea has to give up her own baby for her Mama to raise. I thought she'd die to lose that child. It about crushed her.

POPEYE

Popeye rambles on to Delmont (the man she has fallen hopelessly in love with) in a desperate attempt to connect with him.

Are you writing poems? Carnelle said you write poems. I'd like to read them. (*She starts to run on.*) Course, I never read many poems before. There weren't all that many poem books you could get off a the traveling book mobil. Most books I got was about animals. Farm animals, jungle animals, arctic animals and such. Course they was informative, I learned some things; they's called: a gaggle a geese; a pride a lions; a warren a rabbits; a host a whales. That's my personal favorite one: a host a whales! (*They look at each other.*) Carnelle says you can wiggle your ears. I would have liked t'have seen it. What d'ya dream about at nights? Your face looks tired. I thought maybe you was having bad dreams.

ELAIN

Elain revels in her renewed sense of being an acclaimed beauty and tries to impart some of her expert knowledge to her inept cousin, Carnelle.

Will you just look up at that sky! It's blue as the mighty sea! Oh, I feel like a child today! I swear, I do! You'll never believe it, but Miss Blue has asked me to come up and give a speech before the contest starts. She wants me to talk on, "My Life as a Beauty." Isn't it too exciting!

Oh, Carnation, I went over to Miss Lily's Dress Shop and heard the most disheartening news: poor, little Popeye was fired yesterday afternoon. They said she was giving away the merchandise.

But anyway, I came up with the most creative idea to save the day. You can wear this lovely Mardi Gras mask in the opening parade. That way you can just hold it up to your face like this, covering the side of your dress where the extra material is with your arm and elbows, plus adding some mystery and elegance to—well, to your total look. Just walk around like this.(*She moves around making dips and swirls, alternately moving the mask from in front of her face to the side of it with a flip of her wrist, as she makes her dips.*) And scoop! And Scoop! And Scoop! You think you can manage it? Just flip out your wrist. Make it crisp!

It's amazing but everyone recognizes me. They say I'm still exactly the same as I was. "Just in full bloom like a rose!" That's what one dear man said. I wish mama were here. She'd love all of this!

POPEYE

Popeye relates the story of her abrupt dismissal from Miss Celia Lilly's dress shop.

I reckon what it was was when I was sewing up there in the front a the big store. This little child walked in and she started looking in at all the shiny jewelry behind the glass counter. I saw her looking and I said, "My, what lovely eyes you have. Them's pretty eyes. What color are them eyes?" And she looks up at me and say, "I don't know. I don't have no idea."

Well, I gets out this compact case from behind the glass counter. It's covered with the most beautiful colored sea shells in all the world. And I give it to her and says, "Look in there and tell me what color your eyes is." She takes a long look and says, "Them's blue eyes." And that was the truth, she was right about it. So I give her the sea shell compact case to take on with her, just by chance she forgets what color her eyes is and needs to take a look. Well, Miss Celia Lilly comes looking for that compact case later on in the day. I told her what happened and that's when she give me the news, "Popeye, you're fired."

THE WAKE OF JAMEY FOSTER
(Set in Canton, Mississippi.)

The Wake of Jamey Foster was presented at the Eugene O'Neill Theatre, in New York City, on October 14, 1982. It was directed by Ulu Grosbard. The cast was as follows:

Marshall Foster	Susan Kingsley
Leon Darnell	Stephen Tobolowsky
Katty Foster	Belita Moreno
Wayne Foster	Anthony Heald
Collard Darnell	Patricia Richardson
Pixrose Wilson	Holly Hunter
Brocker Slade	Brad Sullivan

KATTY

Katty tries to suppress her fury and be helpful to her in-law Collard who has shown up for Jamey's funeral dressed in a mud-covered gown.

Well, I just don't know what you're gonna wear. The people will be arriving from ten this morning on. Do you think you could find something of Marshael's that might be suitable? You see, the only clothes I brought are strictly organized. I mean, I'm wearing this outfit all day today, and then tomorrow I'm wearing my navy blue suit with my navy pumps and my navy dress hat with the white piping. But of course now, if you feel you could fit into my navy outfit, I suppose you could wear it today. I mean, you're welcome to try it. (*Following her.*) I could wash and iron it out tonight so I could still wear it tomorrow morning for the funeral. That is if Marshael has all the cleaning apparatus that I'll be needing.

(*Pause.*) We're all overwrought. (*Pause.*) Reverend Rigby says sudden violent deaths are the most difficult to deal with.

PIXROSE

Pixrose explains why she does not like fires.

I've been afflicted by fire most of my entire life. It started out my mamma hating the house we lived in. She used t'say it was trashy. She'd sit around in the dark holding lit matches—always threatening to burn this trashy house down—and one day she did it. She lit up the dining room curtains, loosing flames over the entire house and charcoaling herself to death as a final result.

It's a terrible crime, arson. Caused me t'get burns all over the lower parts of my body. (*Pulling at her stockings.*) I can cover up the scars by wearing these leg stockings. I just wish my arms hadn't caught fire in the automobile explosion. I used t'like to look at 'em. But, of course, my daddy, he died an instantaneous death, and my brother, frankly suffered permanent brain damage; so I guess I was just lucky t'be flung burning from outta the car. That explosion was also diagnosed as deliberate arson.

Arson...It's a terrible, terrible crime.

MARSHAEL

Marshael expresses her horribly mixed feelings for her deceased husband, Jamey.

(*After staring at the closet she opens it and takes out Jamey's suit.*) There. Here it is. His blue pin-striped suit. I liked it best, and here I am holding it, but somehow I don't feel a tear in this world. It's like a hole's been shot through me, and all my insides have been blown out somewhere else. (*She gets a brush and starts brushing the suit.*) I just wish I knew what I felt for Jamey. First one thing, I guess, and then another, I sure wish I knew. It haunts me not to know. (*She continues to brush the suit.*) He did things different. I remember one time he brought this huge, ugly, fat boy home with him about supper time. Jamey whispered that he'd found the fat boy crying in the road 'cause his only pet bird had flown away and could I please fix blueberry muffins for desert. He kissed my fingers when I said I would. (*She crosses to the hall door and hangs up the suit.*) He had dreams though. And it's hard being involved with a man whose dreams don't get fulfilled.

He wanted to be a great world-wide historian. He used to have all sorts of startling revolutionary ideas about the development of mankind that he kept trying to write into books and theories. We sometimes played this game where we'd spin this globe around. (*Spin.*) Saying like, "We're gonna go...there!" (*She yells out the name of the country her finger actually lands on.*) Or, "We're taking a banana boat (*Spin.*) to...here!" (*She looks down and reads the name.*) Then we'd imagine how it would be when we arrived. (*She sits on the chest.*) It was a fun game, but we stopped playing after he had to take that awful job in real estate. (*She spins the globe around and around. She stops the globe with her finger and says the name of the country it lands on.*) I was afraid to ask him for anything. I never wanted him to know how scared I was. I just kept on telling him how, until all his theories were finished and started selling, that real estate was fine with me. I wanted so badly for things to be right for us. My parents fought all the time when I was little. Yelling and crying in the night. I wanted a different kind of life; but it didn't work out.

It seemed the harder I tried the less he cared. The more he blamed me and the children for his dreams not coming true, I thought maybe it would help, if we just knew one way or the other about his work. That's why I sent it off to the publishers. When he found out, he was gone. Went off to live with that fat yellow-haired woman. And now he's really gone. He's out of the whole deal; and I don't even know what we felt for each other. Stupid. Lord. My mouth aches.

PIXROSE

Late at night, Pixrose tells of the loss of her child in a dream.

I've never actually been pregnant. I guess 'cause I'm, well, I'm still a virgin. But I was pregnant one time in a dream. And when the child was born he was half human and half sheep and they said he was to be sold as a slave. But before they took him, I was allowed to hold him in my arms. His body was so warm and soft. I felt his heart beating against my heart. Then I looked down at his small sheeplike face, and he was crying. Then they took him away to become a slave.

MARSHAEL

Marshael rages at Jamey for his betrayal and desertion. By doing so, she releases her pained love and discovers that, even though Jamey is no more, an element of their love was real and imperishable.

(*The lights focus on Marshael's room. She is talking to herself and putting Jamey's clothes in a sack.*) All these ties. You never wore even half of 'em. Wasted ties. God, loose change. Always pockets full of loose change. And your Spearmint chewing gum sticks. Damn, and look—your lost car keys. Oh, well, the car's gone now. Damn you, leaving me alone with your mess. Leaving me again with all your goddamn, gruesome mess t'clean up. Damn, you, wait! You wait! You're not leaving me here like this. You're gonna face me! I won't survive! You cheat! I've got t'have something...redemption...something.

(*She leaves the room, goes down to the parlor and walks in. The coffin is closed. She begins to circle it.*) There you are. Coward. Hiding. Away from me. Hiding. (*Moving in on him.*) Look, I know I hurt you something bad, but why did you have to hold her fat, little hand like that? Huh? Treating me like nothing! I'm not...nothing. Hey, I'm talking. I'm talking to you. You'd better look at me. I mean it, you bastard! (*She pulls the lid off the coffin.*) Jamey. God, your face. Jamey, I'm scared. I'm so scared. I'm scared not to be loved. I'm scared for our life not to work out. It didn't, did it? Jamey? Damn you, where are you? Are you down in Moblie, baby? Have you taken a spin to Moblie? I'm asking you—shit— Crystal Springs? How 'bout Scotland? You wanted to go there...your grandfather was from there. You shit! You're not...I know you're not...I love you! God. Stupid thing to say. I love you! Okay, okay. You're gone. You're gone. You're not laughing. You're not...nothing. (*She moves away from the coffin, realizing it contains nothing of value.*) Still I gotta have something. Still something...(*As she runs out of the parlor then out the front door.*) The trees. Still have the trees. The purple, purple trees—

THE DEBUTANTE BALL
(Set in Hattiesburg, Mississippi.)

VIOLET

Violet remembers the time she saw a host of escaped parrots shrieking and flying through the trees. The birds were a sign to her that it was time for change.

I was just thinking 'bout the time when I heard them birds. First I thought it was some wild child crying. So I went outside in the pouring rain t'hunt for it and then flapping up outta the trees I saw all them colors flying. The most beautiful colors alive—just coming up outta them trees in the drowning rain. All them lost birds shrieking this sad, mournful cry like there ain't nothing left but dying. My mama come and tol' me that them was tropical parrot birds and they liked t'mimic the talk they hear. It always stuck with me wondering, 'bout where they would of heard such mournful crying t'recollect.

TEDDY

Teddy, the debutante, confesses one of her many dark secrets to Violet.

I'm not a belle. Mama, she wanted me to go to that ball and be a belle. But me, I'm no belle. Awhile ago, see, I was staying by myself at an old hotel up in Oxford, Mississippi. After supper one night I got on the elevator to ride up to my room. And just as the doors were about to close, a man stepped inside to ride up with me. I glanced over and saw his left arm was cut off right above the elbow. He wore a short-sleeved shirt and you could see the scarred nub. Then

I caught sight of his face where the whole side of it was just...missing. I felt sick and sticky, and wanted to get off the ride. My legs buckled out from under me; he reached his good arm out to help me. But I said to him, "You get away from me, you ugly man." Then the elevator stopped. The doors opened. But he didn't move. He just stayed hovering over in a corner with this weepy cry coming from the inside his throat.

Violet, remember that baby I spoke to you about? It's his baby. I kinda just did it to be polite. I was at a point, you see, where I just couldn't take on any more, ah, bad feelings, guilt. Just no more. After we did it he said to me, "Mm-mm good." Can you believe it? "Mm-mm good." I still smell him on my skin sometimes.

JEN

After a disastrous evening at the ball, Jen rails against her oldest daughter Bliss who has always felt unfairly neglected.

Neglect you? I neglect you? Well, please, let us not forget about little Butterball when we speak of neglected children. When was the last time you saw your child? What did you send her for her birthday? I never once have forgotten *your* birthday. Although I wish to God I could! You! You think I could be jealous of you! You dream you're some beautiful lady, but you're nothing but a Southern strumpet whore! You bring all your filthy baggage to intrude on my life, but I'm throwing you out! Out! Do you hear me! Out! Out! You're an unproductive being! A worthless mis-creation! You're cheap! Cheap! Cheap! Maybe I'm not a very good mother. Maybe I never should have had any children after all.

BLISS

With no place to go and no one to care for her, Bliss makes a late-night phone call to her former husband, asking him if she can come back home.

(*Into the phone.*) Yes, hello? Is this Tommy?...Well, hi, this is Blissy. I'm, oh, just visiting here in town for a while...Yes, right, for Teddy's Debutante Ball. So did Butterball—did she know I was going to the ball?...Oh, well, anyway tell her I'm going to give her the jeweled princess's crown I received as a party favor. I want her to have it...Listen, Tommy, could I, ah, could I come see you sometime?...Well, it's just, I—I miss you and Butterball an awful lot, and I'd really like to maybe—try and come back home...Right. Well, of course, I know it's very difficult to live with me day in and day out...it's just I can't seem to make it on my own. My last employer accused me of lying about graduating from high school. He said I couldn't make change properly. I've got to tell you, I just don't know what's going to become of me...Yes. Certainly I understand how you feel...Uh-huh. I see...No, really it was just a— fleeting fancy I had. You see, it occurred to me that

I'd be able to teach Butterball how to tell time and tie her shoe. I didn't learn how to do those two things until very late and I remember feeling so badly about it...You will? Well, good then. That's very good. So, Tommy, goodbye. (*Bliss puts the phone down.*)

(*With a laugh.*) Oh, well, maybe it was a mistake sleeping with every one of his friends before leaving the state.

TEDDY

Teddy tells her stepfather, Hank, what happened the night her father was murdered.

(*Putting jam on her toast.*) Daddy broken into the house really crazy that evening. He kept yelling about how he was gonna break Mama all up; cut her to stringy pieces. Seems he'd just found out about her filing for divorce. I served him some coffee and turnip greens, trying to calm him down. But then he slings the sugar bowl at my chest and starts screaming about how there's not enough sugar, it's not full enough and he's sick of scraping the bottom of the bowl—and he's gonna scrape the bottom of her bowl with this switchblade knife he pulls out. Well, I go to get a broom to clean up the sugar, but then I hear Mama's car. He hears it too and stops yelling and just sits silently eating turnip greens off the blade of his knife. The car door slams and I hear Mama coming up the walk, that's when I just grab the black skillet and walk back over and smash his skull. To stop him. Just stop him till she can run away. That's all I wanted—to let her run away.

I cry sometimes thinking how little I miss him.

THE LUCKY SPOT
(Set in Pigeon, Louisiana. Christmas Eve, 1934.)

The Lucky Spot was presented by Manhattan Theatre Club at City Center Theatre in New York City on April 9, 1987. It was directed by Stephen Tobolowsky. The cast was as follows:

Cassidy Smith	Mary Stuart Masterson
Turnip Moss	Alan Ruck
Reed Hooker	Ray Baker
Whitt Carmichael	Lanny Flaherty
Lacey Rollins	Belita Moreno
Sue Jack Tiller Hooker	Amy Madigan
Sam	John Wylie

SUE JACK

Sue Jack has just been released from the Angola State Penitentiary. This is the first time she has seen her husband, Reed Hooker, in three years. She wants to convince him that she has changed so he will take her back.

I'm not the same as I was, Reed. Go on and look at me. You see, I'm not the same. I'm not the same one who kept on hurting you by drinking, and brawling and gambling it all away. And I'm not the young, laughing girl you married with the rosy cheeks and pretty hands. I guess I'm not sure who I am. And, I tell you, it's been making me feel so strange. When I was in prison, the only belonging I had was this old photograph of myself that was taken just before I ran off from home. In it I'm wearing this straw hat decorated with violets and my hair's swept back in a braid and my eyes, they're just...shining...I used to take out that picture and look at it. I kept on pondering over it. I swear it confused me so much, wondering where she was—that girl in the picture. I could not imagine where she'd departed to—so unknowingly, so unexpectedly. (*A pause.*) Look, I won't drink or yell or fight or shoot pool or bet the roosters or—

Please. I don't wanna lose any more. I'm through throwing everything away with both fists.

SUE JACK

Sue Jack has discovered that, while she was in prison, her husband impregnated Cassidy Smith, a fifteen-year-old waif. Sue Jack strongly refutes Cassidy's claim that Hooker intends to divorce Sue Jack so that he can wed Cassidy.

If he told you he'd marry ya, then he's a no good dirt-crawling liar. See 'cause he's never gonna marry you. He can't. He's married to me. Now you listen to me, you greasy little runt. He's my husband. He loves me. He can't help it. (*Sue Jack picks up the shotgun and aims it in Cassidy's direction.*) And if I were you, I wouldn't go around spreading lies that that. Understand, I'm never gonna get over loving Reed Hooker. 'Cause even when I don't know who in this godless world I am, or was, or ever will be—the one thing I know as sure as the smell of spring rain is that I utterly, hopelessly love that rotten, worthless son of a bitch! (*Throughout the following, Sue Jack fires the shotgun shattering a mirror, light fixtures and the jukebox.*) I want, want, want him like a crazy shrieking, howling dog. I can't live without him! I'll blow out my brains. I'll shoot you to pieces. I'll rip this fucking place t' the ground. But, by God, I gotta have that miserable, lying, double-crossing, one and only love of my broken life! (*Sue Jack stops firing the gun. She looks around a moment then stumbles across the room and gets the whiskey bottle.*) Oh God, look here. I've been misering the bottle. I didn't mean t' do that.

CASSIDY

Cassidy, who is eight months pregnant with Hooker's child, talks to Hooker's estranged wife Sue Jack in an attempt to explain how is all happened.

Look here, my knees got dirt all on 'em. I have real trouble keeping clean. (*She spits on her hand and starts scrubbing her knees.*) Mr. Pete, he used t' call me a godless bag a stench. Mr. Pete's the man I was with before. He's the one Hooker won me offa. And that was a lucky day for me. See 'cause when I was with Mr. Pete practically all he'd ever give me t' eat was cow feed. Why, if fact be known, the man was downright feeble-minded. Look here where he branded me with his holy cross. (*Cassidy hikes up her skirt and reveals a cross branded to her inner thigh.*) He's always telling me how all fired holy he is. Him being a member of the Church of Innocent Blood—and me being a godless bag a stench. Lord, my life ain't never been no good till now. But here, well, we have supper together every night. It's the most I ever felt like a family.

Look, I just wanted t' tell ya—it wasn't like what you was saying this morning. See Hooker, he wasn't all mean and drunk or nothing like that the night when it happened.

See used to be I'd hear him at night yelling out and gasping for air and such. I reckoned him t' be having bad dreams; so I started rushing down t' his room t' wake him up. I'd bring him water t' drink and wet down his forehead with a cool rag. Afterward he'd never go back t' sleep, but he'd send me back on t' bed telling me how I needed t' get my rest. Then one time he just up and says for me t' stop coming in with the water. Says for me just t' stay put and let him be. And I done that for some nights. I sure didn't like listening t' him, but I stood it. Then this one night I hear such crying, like it's coming from some sick, dying animal. Well, I can't find no control for myself, but t' run in with the water. I wake him up and I wash off his face and I hold him so hard and I say, "Don't be scared no more. I can make ya feel better. I know some ways t' make ya feel better." And I did too, from being on the trail so long with Mr. Pete. Next day though he moves all my things up t' the attic. (*A beat.*) He locks me up there at nights now. Turnip, he'll come by and unlatch the door in the mornings. I'm hoping all that's gonna be changed once we're married. But I don't really know.

CASSIDY

Cassidy explains to Sue Jack that she has broken her engagement to Hooker because she now believes in love and wants to be free to find someone who will truly love her.

Well, I reckon I outta tell ya I broken off my marriage t' Hooker. Tore off the engagement ring. It's gone.

The thing is I can't never awaken no love in him for me—'cause, well, he's got you in his blood; you're his partner.

See I ain't stupid. I know people getting married's supposed to be in love with the people they's getting married to. Ya don't want somebody just marrying ya on the rebound. And it's funny but it makes me feel light-hearted, 'cause now I see, well, maybe love ain't a made-up lie like Santa Claus or something. Maybe it can be true. And if it's true, maybe I can find someone I'll shoot off guns for and find someone who'll hold my face and tell me, please, please, please. Or maybe he'll just, I don't know, give me a slice of watermelon and pick out all the seeds. Why, having this child don't even scare me no more. 'Cause if ya have this love inside ya it don't matter if your father was a lord in a castle or a bum on the road or a murderer in a cage. It don't matter. Well, here's a hat for ya. Merry Christmas.

ABUNDANCE

(Set in the Wyoming Territory and later in St. Louis, Missouri.
The play spans twenty-five years, starting in the late 1860's.)

Abundance was produced by the Manhattan Theatre Club in
New York City, on October 4, 1990. It was directed by Ron
Lagomarsino. The cast was as follows:

Bess Johnson	Amanda Plummer
Macon Hill	Tess Harper
Jack Flan	Michael Rooker
William Curtis	Lanny Flaherty
Elmore Crome	Keith Reddin

Abundance was produced by the South Coast Repertory, Costa
Mesa, California, on April 21, 1989. The cast was as follows:

Bess Johnson	O-Lan Jones
Macon Hill	Belita Moreno
Jack Flan	Bruce Wright
William Curtis	Jimmy Ray Weeks
Elmore Crome	John Walcutt

MACON

Young Macon meets Bess out west at a stagecoach ranch. She seeks to convince Bess that they are beginning a limitless life full of limitless possibilities.

Lord Almighty. You're just like me. Biscuit? Go ahead. Help yourself. What's mine is yours; what's yours is mine. After all, you're like me. You've come out west to see the elephant. To see what's out there; whatever's out there. (*Beat.*) What do you guess is out there?

Could be anything. I savor the boundlessness of it all. The wild flavor. I'm drunk with western fever. Have you ever seen a map of the world? Well, it stopped my heart. There are oceans out there. Oceans aplenty, and I swear to you I'm gonna see one and walk in one and swim in one for sure. I love water, it never stops moving. I want to discover gold and be rich. I want to erect an ice palace and kill an Indian with a hot bullet. I'm ready for some sweeping changes. How about you? We could be friends throughout it all. It's part of our destiny. I can smell destiny. One day I'm gonna write a novel about it all and put you in it.

BESS

Young Bess rambles on to Macon about her fears and hopes concerning her future husband whose arrival she is anxiously awaiting.

I—I'm hoping my husband ain't gonna be real terrible ugly. It don't mention nothing about his looks in the matrimonial ad.

'Course I know I'm no prize. I got nice hair, but my eyes are too close together and my nerves are somewhat aggravated. Still, I was hoping we'd be in love like people in them stories. The ones about princesses and chimney sweeps and dragon slayers. I don't know, I—well, I'll bet he's gonna be like me some.

I promise I'll be a good wife, patient and submissive. If he'd only come. I hope he ain't forgotten. He sent partial fare. Three letters and partial fare. Three letters all about the size of the western sky. And he loves singing. I can sing real pretty. Oh, I'm betting we're gonna be a match made in heaven, if only I ain't left stranded. See, 'cause, well, I don't know how I'll get by. I can't do nothing. I don't know nothing. I oughta know something by now. I went t'school. They must have taught me something there. But I can't even recall what my favorite color is. Maybe it's blue, but I'm just guessing.

BESS

Starving and freezing to death, Bess struggles to tell her violent husband, Jack, about the death of their beloved Prairie Dog.

You know what, Jack? Jack, you know what? I think it's Christmas. I've been thinking that all day. I could be wrong. But I might be right. There's not much wheat in all this straw. Not much wheat to speak of. Would you agree it could be Christmas?

Of course, Macon would have been here by now if it'd been Christmas. She was planning to bring us a galore of a spread. I was looking forward to it. Maybe the bad weather's put her off. The blizzards. Blinding blizzards for weeks now. Keeping Christmas from our front door. Jack, something happened to Prairie Dog. It was when you went out trying to kill us something this morning. This man came by. Some wandering sort of vagabond dressed in rags. Dirt rags. He wanted a handout. Food, you know.

I sent him on his way, "We don't have anything," I said. "I gotta go through the straw in the bed mattress picking out slivers of wheat so we won't starve here to death. I don't have food to spare some unknown wanderer." He asked me for just a cup of warm water, but I said no. Not because we couldn't spare it, but just because I didn't want him around here on the premises anymore. Something about him. His face was red and dirty. His mouth was like a hole. (*About the wheat.*) This is not gonna be enough for supper, this right here.

As he, as the vagabond was leaving, Prairie Dog followed after him barking. He picked up a stone and grabbed her by the throat and beat her head in with it. With the rock. She's out back in a flour sack. I'd burn her ashes, if only we could spare the wood.

BESS

Bess, who is miserable in her loveless marriage, fights to convince her friend, Macon, that it is time for them to desert their husbands and head west together.

The list is complete. Completely complete. The day has arrived. The time has come. We have it all here; tallow, rice, tea, chip beef, grease bucket, water barrel, one kettle, one fry pan, powder, lead shot— Check it out. See for yourself. The list is complete.

You swore last time soon as I got the new items on the list we'd go. Please, I can't stay here no longer.

I try not to show my hurt. I hide it in different parts of the house. I bury jars of it in the cellar; throw buckets of it down the well; iron streaks of it into the starched clothes and hang them in the closet. I just can't hide it no more. We got t'go now. You promised. You swore.

SIGNATURE
(Set in L. A. in the year 2052.)

L-TIP

L-Tip, a housewife turned manager, expounds on her newfound philosophy that trend is the key to life.

(*Tearing a vail off her dress.*) I've got this theory. I've developed it. Trend is life.

If you're doing what's doing now, at least you know you're doing something. Even if it's stupid and fleeting, dangerous and dull, at least it's happening. There's assurance in knowing you are participating in an era.

Before I had this theory, I wasn't anybody. All I knew about myself was I was in my thirties, I was Max's wife, I worked at a noodle stand, and Chee Chee Kitty was my favorite Fantasy Puppet. I had all the Chee Chee Kitty fashion attire, laser dots, kitchen equipment, toiletries.

The thing is, all that stuff doesn't make you happy, 'cause you're still sitting on the sidelines. I ultimately realized, what I really wanted to be doing was all the things the real Chee Chee Kitty was doing on Celeb Bites—wearing outfits made of sugar stars, lapping up the limelight, dancing at Cafe Who's Who with Count Tidbit. So, for the first time, I decided to turn my life around and become a manager. It thrills me knowing what I want, going out and getting it, taking it, swallowing it whole, wiping my lips and coming back for more. Mmm.

WILLIAM

William, a young woman who works cleaning up toxic splatter, talks to C- Boy, a mute government ward, about how to get by in the world.

Hi. I'm William Smit. Do you talk? No? What was it, the drugs that got ya? That's a nice belt. It's orange. Red and yellow together make orange. I know that 'cause it's my favorite color, orange. They say the sun is orange. My suit is orange. My favorite food is an orange. I give myself an orange every Holiday Day. Maybe that sounds strange to you, someone giving their own selves a present. But I believe on occasions it's worthwhile to do nice things for one's self. For instance, I always try and keep my shoes nice and buffed. That way I know I always got something shiny to look at as I'm walking down strange roads that may not be going my way.

L-TIP

L-Tip, who has become a famous celebrity, tells William (a young woman) about her beautiful new baby.

I—Did you know I have a child now? Yes, I've been desperate for one for along time. Here, I'll click her up. (*She Clicks through her number.*) Her name's Grace. (*Into her TVP.*) Yes, H. K., please put Grace on the TVP.

Isn't she the cutest and most cuddly. She's the newest thing. They call them Toss 'Em Toddlers. Her

natural life span is only three years. Isn't it wonderful. She'll be adorable her whole life. And I won't ever have to worry about those awkward years. Not to mention the high cost of education.
(L-Tip waves goodbye to Grace and clicks her off.)

It's all completely natural. See, I don't have time for a full-term child. I mean, I'm competing in a world where fantasy puppets set the step. They never take time out for children or family, ultra surgery or even rehab. They're completely consumed with constructing careers. The pressure gets to be devastating. Of course, I'm terrifically unhappy. Before I started going to my therochief I never even suspected how unhappy I was. Now I am totally aware of my misery. It's a big improvement.

ORDER DIRECT

MONOLOGUES THEY HAVEN'T HEARD. Karshner. Modern speeches written in the language of today. $6.95.

MORE MONOLOGUES THEY HAVEN'T HEARD. Karshner. More exciting living-language speeches. $6.95.

SCENES THEY HAVEN'T SEEN. Karshner. Fresh. contemporary scenes for men and women. $6.95.

FOR WOMEN, MONOLOGUES THEY HAVEN'T HEARD. Pomerance. Contemporary speeches for actresses. $6.95

MONOLOGUES for KIDS. Roddy. 28 wonderful speeches for boys and girls. Modern, incisive. $6.95.

MORE MONOLOGUES for KIDS. Roddy. More great speeches for boys and girls. $6.95.

SCENES for KIDS. Roddy. 30 scenes for girls and boys. $6.95.

MONOLOUGUES for TEENAGERS. Karshner. Contemporary speeches written in language that is *now*. $6.95.

SCENES for TEENAGERS. Karshner. Scenes relevant to today's teenage boys and girls. $6.95.

HIGH SCHOOL MONOLOGUES THEY HAVEN'T HEARD. Karshner. Contemporaty speeches for high schoolers. $6.95.

DOWN HOME MONOLOGUES. Karshner. Speeches in the language of rural America. $6.95.

MONOLOGUES from the CLASSICS. ed. Karshner. Speeches from Shakespeare, Marlowe & others. $6.95.

SCENES from the CLASSICS. ed. Maag. 8 famous scenes from William Shakespeare & others. $6.95.

MONOLOGUES from RESTORATION PLAYS. ed. Maag. A ready reference to great speeches from the period. $6.95.

SHAKESPEARE'S MONOLOGUES THEY HAVEN'T HEARD. ed. Dotterer. Lesser known speeches from The Bard. $6.95.

MONOLOGUES from CHEKHOV. trans. Cartwright. Modern translations from Chekhov's major plays. $6.95.

MONOLOGUES from GEORGE BERNARD SHAW. ed. Michaels. Great speeches from the works of G.B.S. $6.95.

MONOLOGUES from OSCAR WILDE. ed. Michaels. The best of Wilde's urbane, dramatic wirting. $6.95.

WOMAN. Susan Pomerance. Monologues for actresses. $6.95.

WORKING CLASS MONOLOGUES. Karshner. Speeches from blue collar occupations. $6.95.

MODERN SCENES for WOMEN. Pomerance. Contemporary scenes for today's actressess. $6.95.

MONOLOGUES from MOLIERE. trans. Dotterer. A difinitive collection of speeches from the French Master. $6.95.

SHAKESPEARE'S MONOLOGUES for WOMEN. trans. Dotterer. $6.95.

DIALECT MONOLOGUES. Karshner/Stern. 13 essential dialects applied to contemporary monologues. Book & Tape. $19.95.

YOU SAID A MOUTHFUL. Karshner. Tongue twisters galore. Great exercises for actors and singers. $6.95.

TEENAGE MOUTH. Karshner. Modern monologues for teenagers. $6.95.

SHAKESPEARE'S LADIES. Dotterer. A second book of Shakespeare's monologues for women. $6.95.

BETH HENLEY:MONOLOGUES FOR WOMEN. Henley. $6.95.

Your check or money order (no cash or C. O. D.) plus handling charges of $2.50 for the first book, and $1.50 for each additional book. California residents add 81/4 %. Send orders to: Dramaline Publications, 10470 Riverside Drive. Suite #201. Toluca Lake. CA 91602.